Vaccines Explained

The Wholistic Vet's Guide to Vaccinating Your Dog

Laurie S. Coger, DVM, CVCP

This book is not intended as a substitute for the
recommendations of a veterinarian who has
examined your dog. The reader is advised to
consult a veterinarian on a regular basis in regard
to all matters pertaining to his or her dog's health.

ISBN:0615650422
ISBN-13:978-0615650425

DEDICATION

Primum non nocere – first, do no harm.

For those who adhere to this primary principle of medicine, and strive to learn how to better use vaccines for our dogs' health.

And, for those dogs who have suffered adverse reactions from vaccines, and the owners who are left with the heartbreak of loss, or the strain of managing vaccine - induced disease.

ACKNOWLEDGMENTS

Many people and dogs have contributed to my completion of this book. I would like to thank the owners who have entrusted their dogs' care to me, and challenged me to learn more. I am also very grateful for my community of "dog people", who have shared their experiences and knowledge over the years.

This book would have been a never-ending project were it not for the inspiration and support of Lorin Beller, her Big Fish Nation program, and my coach Nancy Duncan.

I'm very grateful for the support of everyone at Bloomingrove Veterinary Hospital. I am fortunate to work with such a dedicated group of compassionate professionals, and a wonderfully diverse and caring group of owners.

In my experience, everyone who chooses to travel down a holistic path has one person who is instrumental in that journey. I am profoundly grateful to Mary Ferentino for showing a very traditional veterinarian other ways to think, all those years ago… From training to natural diet to complementary and alternative health, her knowledge, support, and friendship have been priceless gifts.

CONTENTS

"Dogs are not our whole life, but they make our lives whole." - Roger Caras

Introduction

I see a lot of dogs in my typical workday. Some sick, some healthy, many somewhere in between. I sometimes remember a few details about them after their appointments, but there are a few dogs that are forever vividly etched in my memory. This is the case with Lucy, a 4 month old black Labrador mix adopted from a local rescue group.

Lucy was my 9:15 appointment on an early fall Saturday morning, over eight years ago. It was a beautiful day, and I was looking forward to meeting a friend for lunch and then spending some time with my own dogs. Lucy had been with her owners a few weeks, and was a typical happy, active puppy. She had received her first vaccination (DAPP) four weeks ago while with her foster family. My physical examination revealed no abnormalities – she appeared completely healthy. So I administered her second DAPP vaccination, which happened to be exactly the same brand and formulation she had received a month ago.

Before I could withdraw the needle from her skin, it was apparent that something was very wrong. Lucy stiffened, and then collapsed. I immediately began treatment for this vaccine reaction, and she responded initially. She had her first seizure half an hour later. Over the course of the morning, her seizures progressed, and she stopped responding to the intravenous fluids and drugs we administered. She died at 2:16 PM, just over five hours after she bounced into the hospital, a bright, happy puppy with a tennis ball in her mouth.

I share this story not to make you afraid of vaccines, but rather to point out what potent medical products they are. Vaccines are too often thought of as a minor or routine thing, when the opposite is actually true. The majority of dogs I see in my everyday practice are over-vaccinated, which not only does not benefit them, but also raises numerous health risks.

My purpose in writing this book is to provide a straightforward explanation of what a vaccine is, how it works, and which are (and are not) needed for most dogs. This information is what I want to share with every new puppy owner at his or her first office call (and now that it is in book form I can!). As such, it is intended to be an understandable yet not "dumbed down" explanation of this important medical procedure for every concerned dog owner. You will notice scientific references sprinkled throughout the chapters, as well as in the References section. More technical information is available at the book website, ***www.VaccinesExplained.com*** for those interested. My basic vaccination schedule and "Best Practices" for vaccinating are also included. I sincerely hope this guide aids you in making informed vaccine choices for your dog.

CHAPTER 1. HOW VACCINES WORK

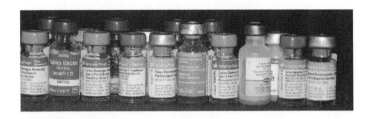

Vaccines have long been used in humans and animals, and have saved countless lives. From smallpox to tetanus to rabies, vaccines have protected our pets, our food animals, and us. When new diseases or strains have emerged, vaccines have been updated to keep pace with new threats. Today's vaccines are extremely potent, and can produce high levels of protective immunity with just a single dose.

There are two main types of vaccines, killed and infectious, (also called modified live), classified by the antigen type they contain. An antigen is a substance that stimulates production of antibodies by the immune system. Antibodies bind to disease causing bacteria or viruses and prevent them from causing disease. Common antigens include killed whole or partial bacteria or viruses, and modified viruses. In a killed vaccine, such as all rabies vaccines, the virus has been deactivated and is unable to cause the disease. In infectious or modified live vaccines (MLV), the virus has been weakened so it cannot cause disease, but can still reproduce in the dog's body. This vaccine type, because it reproduces in the dog's body much as the actual disease causing organism does, can produce a much longer lasting immunity than a killed vaccine.

Vaccines work by stimulating the immune system to produce antibodies to the disease in question. As the vaccine exposes the body to an antigen, the body reacts by producing B-lymphocytes, capable of producing antibodies, along with memory cells. It is important to understand that the vaccine does not immediately give the dog immunity. <u>Vaccines provide a blueprint for the immune system to use in building up healthy defenses against diseases</u>.

The part of the immune system that enables vaccines to work for long periods of time is the memory cell. These cells carry the "imprint" of the disease-causing organism -- for example, parvovirus. Should your dog be exposed to parvovirus years after being vaccinated, these memory cells will reproduce very rapidly, and stimulate swift antibody production and activation of other white blood cell defenses. The end result is that your dog does not get the disease. Many memory cell lines survive for a dog's lifetime.

In order to maximize the chances that the body produces adequate antibodies and memory cells, a dog typically is given two doses of vaccine, separated by four weeks. When the initial vaccine is given, the immune system responds by producing some antibodies and some memory cells. This effect is at its peak two to three weeks after the vaccination is given. When a follow up (booster) dose of the same vaccine is given four weeks after the initial dose, the body responds at a much higher level, with abundant antibody production and proliferation of memory cells. It is important to note that today's extremely effective infectious or modified live vaccines (MLV), which reproduce in the dog's body much as the disease-causing virus would, can produce protective immunity in one dose, according to Dr. Ron Schultz of the University of Wisconsin's Veterinary College.

Vaccines contain other ingredients in addition to antigen. The liquid portion is usually sterile saline. Additives such as thimersol (mercury), formaldehyde, and/or antibiotics are added to preserve and stabilize the vaccine. Some vaccines contain adjuvants, such as aluminum, which enhance the immune system's response. Small amounts of the culture material used to grow the virus or bacteria used in the vaccine, such as egg protein may also be present. The total volume of most vaccines is one milliliter, which is equivalent to 1/5 teaspoon.

It is important to note that commercial vaccine products may cover one or more diseases. Most veterinarians utilize combination vaccines, covering anywhere from three to seven diseases. These products are commonly referred to as a "distemper vaccine" as distemper is usually the first disease named, which can lead to some confusion on the part of owners who don't realize how many antigens are contained in a given vaccine product. Typical combinations include:

DAP - Distemper, adenovirus, parvovirus

DAPP - Distemper, adenovirus, parvovirus, parainfluenza

DAPPC - Distemper, adenovirus, parvovirus, parainfluenza, coronavirus

DAPPC/L - Distemper, adenovirus, parvovirus, parainfluenza, cornonavirus, leptospirosis

It is vital to know exactly which combination is being given to your dog. As you can see, many antigens can be combined into one vaccine, some of which may not be necessary or beneficial for your dog. Do not hesitate to ask to review the label from the vaccine vial before it is given to your dog. Do not allow more than a three antigen combination to be given to your dog (i.e., DAP). Vaccines containing multiple antigens are associated with a higher risk of adverse reactions by some experts. (More specific recommendations are contained in Chapter 5.)

In addition to combinations, some vaccines are available individually, as what are termed single antigen vaccines. Distemper, rabies, and parvovirus are commonly obtainable as single antigens. Many veterinary hospitals do not routinely stock single antigen vaccines, but that does not mean they would be unwilling to order them if requested.

Now that you have a basic understanding of how vaccines work, you are probably wondering about the vaccines your dog has already had, and what ones he will truly need in the future. In the next chapter, you will learn about the diseases from which your dog should be protected, and those that he may not require protection from.

Remember...

1. Vaccines do not give the dog immediate immunity. Instead, they stimulate the production of antibodies that recognize the disease-causing organism and attack it, as well as the production of memory cells that keep the "blueprint" for producing those antibodies.

2. Memory cell lines last many years, in some cases an entire lifetime.

3. Vaccines exist in many combinations – always ask to check the vial to know exactly what your dog is receiving.

CHAPTER 2. CORE VACCINATIONS

Currently, vaccine experts divide vaccinations into two categories: **Core**, or essential vaccines, and **Non-Core**, or special purpose vaccines. I find this greatly simplifies decision making for most owners.

Core vaccines are indicated for virtually every dog. They protect against diseases that the dog is likely to come in contact with, that carry very high mortality risks, or that can be spread to other species including humans. Rabies, distemper, adenovirus, and parvovirus are the core vaccines recognized by the American Animal Hospital Association (AAHA), as well as numerous other veterinary organizations and colleges.

Rabies

Rabies is one of the most deadly viral diseases affecting mammals, including humans. Commonly carried by skunks, raccoons, foxes, and bats, it is virtually always fatal. It is spread by contact with the saliva of an infected animal, typically through a bite. The virus travels from the wound along nerves, eventually reaching the brain, where it causes inflammation, swelling, and loss of normal function. Signs typically include lethargy, loss of coordination, aggression or "dumbness", and seizures. Death follows quickly once these signs begin to occur.

Rabies is generally found in wildlife in the US, although cases in cats, livestock, and occasionally dogs are reported each year. (Humans are rarely infected, and human post exposure treatment is very effective.) Rabid wild animals frequently exhibit abnormal behavioral, whether excessively friendly or calm (the so called "dumb" form of rabies) or extremely aggressive. Animals showing either form can transmit the disease. The common denominator in these cases is that the wild animal is typically out in the daytime, in an area it would not normally be, and is not afraid of humans. Many times rabid animals will wander into populated areas, even getting inside yards. This is a frequent scenario for both dog and human exposure, as neither is aware the rabid animal is in the area until it is too late.

Contact with the saliva of a rabid animal, either directly through a bite, or indirectly by touching the animal or the fur of a dog attacked by a rabid animal is considered an exposure. While the risk is lower than with a bite, virus in saliva present on the fur could gain entrance to the body through cuts or scratches in the skin, or through eyes or mucous membranes. Any possible contact, however minimal, with a possibly rabid animal should be reported to the appropriate medical professional immediately.

Fortunately, today's rabies vaccines are extremely effective. Rabies is the only vaccination that is mandated for dogs by every state in the USA, and most other countries as well. Rabies vaccines exist for most species, including humans who are at significant risk, such as veterinarians, researchers, and animal control officials.

The rabies vaccine is typically given as an initial dose after the puppy is three months of age, and is considered effective for one year. A follow up dose, given one year later, can be considered effective for three years, *provided a three-year approved product is used*. There are a number of products on the market that are labeled for a three-year duration of immunity, as well as others which are labeled for yearly administration. Be sure to verify which vaccine is being given before you approve it.

Because state laws govern rabies vaccination practices, the vaccination schedule differs from that of other vaccines. For example, should a dog be exposed to a rabid animal, state law may require quarantine and revaccination. The length of quarantine and timing of revaccination is in part determined by the date of the dog's last rabies vaccination. It is important to note that dogs not vaccinated against rabies can be ordered euthanized if exposed to a rabid animal. Health department officials, who typically are not veterinarians, and whose first concern is avoiding human health risk, often make this decision. These "unvaccinated dog" scenarios are heartbreaking for all concerned. Keeping your dog's rabies vaccination current is imperative.

Currently research is being done by the Rabies Challenge Fund Charitable Trust to determine the duration of immunity provided by rabies vaccine. Studies have shown dogs are protected, as determined by serum antibody titers, for at least seven years. The goal of the study is to extend the legally required vaccination interval to first five, and then seven years. You can learn more at their website, ***www.RabiesChallengeFund.org***.

Canine Distemper

Canine distemper is caused by a virus related to the human measles virus. It was first described by the French veterinarian Henri Carre' in 1905. The first vaccine was developed in 1950.

The distemper virus spreads both by airborne aerosol droplets and through contact with infected nasal and ocular secretions, feces, and urine. It can also be spread by food and water contaminated with these fluids. Signs of infection include an acute fever, runny nose and eyes, progressing to more severe respiratory and gastrointestinal problems. Encephalomyelitis, an inflammation of the brain and spinal cord, leads to massive convulsions and death. Recovery is possible with treatment, but some dogs are left with long tern neurologic problems.

Fortunately, thanks to the effectiveness of our distemper vaccines, this disease is no longer common in most regions of the USA. It is mainly seen as a sporadic outbreak in stray, unvaccinated dogs or in shelters, where an infected dog can come in contact with many stressed and unvaccinated dogs. Most of today's veterinarians, myself included, have never seen a case of canine distemper. The virus does not live long in the environment, and is easily killed by most cleaners and disinfectants.

Vaccination against distemper has been shown to be protective for many years. In fact, one study showed measurable antibody levels 15 years after vaccination. Given the current practice of rescue groups moving stray or shelter dogs across many states for adoption, the potential for an outbreak exists, and vaccination is recommended.

Parvovirus

Nothing strikes fear into the heart of a dog owner like parvovirus. This highly contagious virus is shed in the stool of infected dogs, and causes profuse vomiting and bloody diarrhea. Puppies are most commonly affected, and often die despite intensive veterinary care with intravenous fluids and medications.

The virus is typically ingested, and it multiplies in the lymphatic system tissues, and then spreads to the bloodstream. It invades rapidly dividing cells, typically those in the lymph nodes, intestinal lining, heart, and bone marrow. The intestinal lining is severely damaged, and bacteria from the intestines cross over into the bloodstream. At the same time, white blood cell numbers are depleted because of lymph node and bone marrow infection. Diarrhea, vomiting, and dehydration are the result of this systemic infection. Mortality can approach 80% in severe cases. Recovered puppies may have long-term damage to their hearts or digestive tracts. Some breeds, such as Dobermans, Pit Bulls, and Rottweilers seem to be more susceptible to infection.

Parvovirus was first recognized in 1978, and spread rapidly around the globe. We saw many cases into the 1990's, when the incidence began to taper off, as vaccine efficacy improved. Our current parvovirus vaccines are extremely effective in preventing infection. We also have several new treatment options and supportive measures should a dog become infected.

In recent years, new strains of the virus have emerged, and have caused much apprehension among both owners and veterinarians. Canine parvovirus type 2 (CPV-2) is the strain that causes the majority of cases of parvovirus enteritis in dogs.

Canine parvovirus type 2c (CPV-2c) is the latest strain of canine parvovirus that has caused concern. It was first detected in Italy in 2000, and has also been reported in Western Europe, Asia, and South America. Outbreaks of canine parvovirus associated with CPV-2c in the United States were confirmed in 2006 and 2007. Fortunately, the parvovirus vaccines in use today have been shown to be effective against this strain.

There are several genetic variations of CPV-2. Internet reports of "new strains" that cause devastating outbreaks of parvo in puppies are common. It is my opinion that these outbreaks are not necessarily new strains, but rather the result of immunologically compromised or incompetent dogs, or incorrectly administered vaccines.

Research reported by Dr. Ron Schultz of the University of Wisconsin Veterinary College revealed that immunity from parvovirus vaccination lasts at least seven years, and protective antibody levels are present for at least nine years.

Adenovirus

There are two types of adenovirus, and they cause two different diseases. Canine adenovirus type 1 (CAV-1) is the cause of infectious canine hepatitis, an acute liver infection. This is a contagious disease that can be found worldwide, but is seldom seen in areas where dogs are commonly vaccinated. It can cause mild to severe disease. The virus is spread feces, urine, blood, saliva, and nasal discharge of infected dogs. Signs include fever, depression, loss of appetite, and abdominal pain. While death may occur, many dogs survive the infection with lasting damage to the eyes and kidneys. Fortunately, the disease is exceedingly rare – in fact, there has not been a reported case of infectious hepatitis in the US in 20 years, according to Dr. Schultz.

Canine adenovirus type 2 (CAV-2) is one of the causes of infectious tracheobronchitis, also known as kennel cough. In most cases of kennel cough, the disease is caused by a combination of viruses and bacteria. (Kennel cough and vaccination against it is discussed in the next chapter.)

Vaccination against Canine Adenovirus type 2 (respiratory) is effective against both types of the virus. This is the most common vaccine in use today, and you may see it listed as "A_2" in a combination vaccine, i.e. DA_2PP. Immunity from this vaccination has been documented to last at least seven years, and protective antibody levels persist for at least nine years.

Remember...

1. Rabies vaccines are legally required, and extremely effective. The Rabies Challenge Fund is working to prove efficacy for 5 and eventually 7 years.

2. Vaccination against distemper likely lasts 7 – 15 years.

3. Current parvovirus vaccines appear to provide cross protection against new strains of the disease.

CHAPTER 3.
NON-CORE & NON-RECOMMENDED VACCINES

Non-core vaccines are special purpose vaccines whose use is determined in light of the exposure risk of the dog -- geographic location, lifestyle, etc. Several of these diseases concerned are self-limiting and/or respond readily to treatment. For various reasons, vaccination with these vaccines is generally less effective in protecting against disease than vaccination with the core vaccines. **Non-recommended vaccines** are classified as such because of insignificance of the disease, lack of efficacy of the vaccine, or a combination of factors.

Kennel Cough: Bordetella and Parainfluenza

Kennel cough is technically known as Infectious tracheobronchitis (ITB). It is a contagious respiratory disease of dogs, often occurring after exposure to other dogs in a boarding kennel or similar situation. Signs include a harsh, hacking, and choking cough. While most cases are mild, some can progress to pneumonia, typically in the very young or old dog, or those weakened by other health problems. Nasal discharge and coughing up of phlegm is often observed. Signs usually develop within a week of exposure.

The disease is caused by a combination of viruses and bacteria, and is spread through the air as infected dogs cough and sneeze. The usual causative organisms are *Bordetella bronchiseptica* and the canine parainfluenza virus, but canine adenovirus, canine respiratory coronavirus, and various bacteria can also be involved. Treatment focuses on suppressing the cough and using antibiotics to address the bacterial component of the infection, while the immune system responds to the viral infection. Most cases resolve in one to two weeks, with the dogs beginning to feel better even sooner.

Vaccination against kennel cough is best done using the intranasal vaccine containing both *Bordetella bronchiseptica* and parainfluenza. This route of vaccination provides quicker and longer lasting protection and requires only one dose. It should be noted that because of the multiple causative agents of kennel cough, vaccination is not a guarantee of protection. In fact, some sources place efficacy of the vaccine at 60 – 70%. Vaccination does lessen or prevent the clinical signs of disease, and in the case of the intranasal vaccine, reduces the chances of spread of disease. You should be aware that many dogs will sneeze and/or cough for many days after receiving the intranasal vaccine.

Boarding kennels, as well as some groomers, daycare, and training facilities commonly require vaccination for kennel cough. If you must have this vaccine given to your dog, it should be administered at least a week before possible exposure for maximum efficacy. It is important to note that, unlike the injectable form of the vaccine, the intranasal vaccine is considered to be effective for 13 – 14 months. Some veterinarians are still recommending administering kennel cough vaccine every six months, but that is inappropriate and unnecessary when using the intranasal vaccine.

Lyme Disease

Lyme disease has become one of the most common tick-transmitted diseases known, reaching almost epidemic proportions in some parts of the country. Caused by the spirochete *Borrelia burgdorferi,* it is spread by ticks, especially the deer tick.

Classic signs are joint swelling and pain, often appearing suddenly. Fever, lethargy, lameness, a hunched stance, and reluctance to move are also common signs. Sometimes signs will be very vague and non-specific. Routine testing in areas where the disease is widespread is common practice. Treatment with the antibiotic doxycycline treats most cases successfully, although a small percentage of dogs will experience relapses or serious kidney disease.

There are currently a few different types of vaccinations available for Lyme. One contains the entire killed spirochete (Fort Dodge/Pfizer Lymevax®), while another contains a portion of the outer surface proteins. (Nobivac Lyme®). A third is a recombinant subunit vaccine, which according to the manufacturer, "By using only pure outer surface protein A (OspA), RECOMBITEK Lyme® provides unsurpassed efficacy... Plus, RECOMBITEK Lyme® contains no chemical adjuvants, thus eliminating the potential risk typically associated with adjuvants." (From Merial® website). The presence of three different types of vaccines reflects the difficulty of producing an effective, non-reactive vaccine against this disease.

Whether or not to vaccinate your dog against Lyme (assuming it is common in your region) is a complex question. Many experts do not encourage vaccination, citing increased risk of reaction with the killed vaccines, and less than optimal efficacy of all types of vaccine. And while the currently available vaccines are better than those of just five years ago, it is still common in my everyday practice to see dogs experiencing adverse reactions, or becoming infected despite vaccination. Lyme vaccine is the most likely vaccine to cause reactions in my practice.

Should you decide it is in your dog's best interest to receive the vaccination, some commonsense procedures should be followed. First, have him for Lyme prior to vaccinating. It is pointless potentially detrimental to vaccinate a dog that is positive for Lyme. Do not give Lyme vaccine in conjunction with any other vaccines. At this time, the least reactive vaccine appears to be the recombinant one, but be sure to research and discuss the vaccine fully with your veterinarian, as our knowledge of the disease grows, and vaccines are refined.

Leptospirosis

Leptospirosis, a bacterial disease caused by infection with bacteria of the *Leptospira* family, affects humans as well as other mammals, birds, amphibians, and reptiles. Fever and depression are often the first signs infected dogs show. Joint or muscle pain and reluctance to move follow. Many dogs have vomiting and diarrhea, and discharge from the eyes and nose. As the disease progresses, the liver and kidneys are affected. The dog may become jaundiced as the liver is damaged, and urination, which was increased, stops as the kidneys are damaged.

Definitive diagnosis of leptospirosis is by laboratory blood testing. The bacteria can be detected in the urine and blood by fluorescent antibody staining. Serological testing, measuring antibody levels to the disease, may also be useful in diagnosing leptospirosis.

Leptospirosis is treatable with antibiotics (usually penicillin or doxycycline) and supportive care. However, the damage done to the liver and kidneys by the bacteria can be permanent. Therefore, many veterinarians will begin aggressive treatment even before test results return if leptospirosis in question. Left untreated, the disease can cause liver and/or kidney failure and death.

So how does a dog become infected with leptospirosis? The bacteria live in the fluids of infected animals (often wild animals and birds), including urine, saliva, blood and milk, and are shed in these fluids. The disease may be carried for years in animals that serve as host reservoirs without the animals showing clinical signs of the disease. *Leptospira* spirochetes are more prevalent in marshy or swamp areas that have stagnant surface water and are contaminated by urine of infected wildlife. The bacteria survive best in neutral or slightly alkaline water or other fluids, and at moderate temperatures (around 77 degrees Fahrenheit). Transmission occurs by direct contact with the fluids or with an infected animal, as well as by indirect contact, including contamination on vegetation, food and water, soil and bedding materials.

While it can be transmitted to people, leptospirosis is rarely seen in humans. (An estimated 100-200 cases are identified annually in the United States, with about 50% of these cases occurring in Hawaii.) Transmission to humans typically occurs by contact with water that has been contaminated by animal urine with unhealed breaks in the skin, the eyes, or mucous membranes. (A fact that vaccine manufacturers' advertisements seem to ignore, as they imply owners will be infected by their dogs unless they are vaccinated.) Given the problems caused by the disease and the zoonotic potential, you might think that vaccination of all dogs would be logical. However, the nature of the disease and the available vaccines make vaccination a more complex issue.

First, there are multiple serovars (strains) of *Leptospira* that cause disease in dogs. Currently available vaccines do not contain all disease causing serovars, and the included serovars do not cross-protect against other serovars. Beyond that, *Leptospira* vaccines do not prevent infection in dogs, but rather minimize the severity of the infection. They also do not prevent the bacteria from invading the dog's kidneys, which means the bacteria can still be shed in the infected dog's urine.

Second, the efficacy of the vaccine against infection with the specific serovar (strain) is between 50 and 75%, and the duration of immunity is probably about 1 year or possibly less. We've known this for some time -- the 2003 American Animal Hospital

Association's Canine Vaccine Guidelines stated, "Immunity is an ill-defined term for Leptospira ssp. products. If immunity is defined as protection from infection or prevention of bacterial-shedding, then there is little or no enduring immunity."

Third, the vaccine is considered by many veterinarians to be among the most reactive. In fact, 2006 American Animal Hospital Association's Canine Vaccine Guidelines, it states, "Veterinarians are advised of anecdotal reports of acute anaphylaxis in toy breeds following administration of leptospirosis vaccines. Routine vaccination of toy breeds should only be considered in dogs known to have a high exposure risk." The incidence of reactions was also noted to be higher in puppies less than 12 weeks of age. Newer sub-unit type vaccines are claimed by manufacturers to be less reactive.

Finally, the incidence of this disease is low. Twenty-one cases of Leptospirosis cases were reported in Los Angeles County (CA) dogs between 2005 and April 2010, with eight deaths. Another study, published in the Journal of the American Veterinary Medical Association, showed a prevalence of the disease in veterinary teaching hospitals to be 0.037% between 1970 and 1998.

Should you decide that vaccination against leptospirosis is in your dog's best interest, you can take some precautions to lessen the risk of adverse reactions. First, be sure your dog is completely healthy at the time of vaccination. Second, do not give leptospirosis vaccine in conjunction with any other vaccine. Use a four-week vaccination interval. Third, do not administer leptospirosis vaccine to puppies under the age of twelve weeks. Fourth, monitor closely after vaccination for any changes in health or behavior that could be signs of a reaction. If changes occur, seek veterinary attention immediately.

Canine Influenza

Canine influenza, commonly called "dog flu" is caused by a Type A influenza virus. The disease affects dogs exclusively. Known to exist in horses, it is theorized that the virus adapted to infect dogs, and is now a dog specific strain. It was first found in dogs in 2004, in a respiratory disease outbreak in Greyhounds.

Symptoms of the disease include a cough, nasal discharge, and fever. It can progress to a severe form, including secondary bacterial infection and pneumonia, especially in dogs with pre-existing problems. However, most dogs (about 80% according to the Center for Disease Control) will have a very mild form which may even be mistaken for kennel cough. It is spread by aerosolized secretions from infected dogs, or by contact with contaminated objects or people.

The available dog flu vaccine is a killed virus vaccine containing an adjuvant, the antibiotic gentamicin, and the antifungal amphoteracin B. The vaccine does not prevent the disease, but rather decreases the incidence and severity of coughing, viral shedding, and lung lesions. It is labeled for use in healthy, non-parasitized dogs, and should not be given to pregnant dogs.

Much publicity accompanied the vaccine's release in 2009. However, reports on the actual numbers of dogs affected are difficult to find. While the vaccine manufacturer reports cases have been found in virtually every state, Dr. Edward Dubovi, Director of Cornell University's Virology Section of the Animal Health Diagnostic Center, noted in December 2011, … "that the increased detection might be the result of heightened awareness and vigilance rather than a real rise in infections. Because no central database exists for canine influenza, information on national disease incidence often is "done off rumor." Clearly, more hard data from impartial sources is needed before this vaccine can be recommended.

Coronavirus

The American Animal Hospital Association classifies canine coronavirus vaccine as a "Not Recommended" vaccine. Their reason for this is the mildness of infection and the fact that "neither the MLV vaccine nor the killed vaccines have been shown to significantly reduce disease caused by a combination of coronavirus and parvovirus. Only canine parvovirus vaccines have been shown to protect dogs against a dual-virus challenge." (2011 AAHA Canine Vaccination Guidelines).

Coronavirus vaccine is available as a single antigen product, or more commonly in combination distemper products. In some areas, these vaccines are heavily promoted. However, the benefits of vaccination are nil. In fact, according to the Veterinary Medical Teaching Hospital at University of California – Davis, "Infection with canine enteric coronavirus (CCV) alone has been associated with mild disease only, and only in dogs < 6 weeks of age. It has not been possible to reproduce the infection experimentally, unless immunosuppressive doses of glucocorticoids are administered." Therefore, I concur with AAHA's classification, and recommend against administering this vaccine.

Remember...

1. Vaccination against Kennel Cough is best done by using an intranasal *Bordetella* and Parainfluenza vaccine.

2. Be sure to test for Lyme prior to vaccinating. Do not vaccinate dogs which test positive for Lyme .

3. Leptospirosis is not as common as advertising may make it appear, and vaccine efficacy and reactivity is a problem.

4. Canine Influenza has been around since 2006, and increased vigilance and more frequent testing of samples may exaggerate the incidence.

CHAPTER 4. TITERS

You may have heard of owners having their dog's blood tested for antibodies as an alternative to vaccinations. This test, called a titer, is a measurement of the dog's antibody level to a specific disease. If a dog has sufficient antibodies, he is considered immune to the disease in question. Vaccinating a dog that already has sufficient antibodies provides absolutely no benefit – he is already protected from the disease.

Titers are expressed as a number, based on the number of times the dog's blood sample can be diluted and antibody still detected. For example, the first test is done on the undiluted sample. The sample is then diluted in half (expressed as 1:2), and tested for antibody. If it is present, that sample is diluted in half (1:4), and so forth. The final result is the greatest dilution value in which antibody can still be detected. Most laboratories today will titer only to what they consider a protective dilution – currently for the widely used veterinary testing service provided by Antech Laboratories® that is 1:5. The theory behind this is that dilution is the minimum that is associated with protection from the disease, and there is no need to go further. Other facilities will titer to an endpoint, giving you a more exact antibody level. Typical endpoints could be 1:256, 1:1024, or more – quite high antibody levels, indeed.

Currently, most experts recommend testing titers for only two diseases, distemper and parvovirus. Not only are these the most serious diseases that we commonly vaccinate against, a protective titer to them demonstrates the competence of the dog's immune system. Titering for other diseases is not necessary.

Many owners inquire about titer tests for Rabies. These are typically done when a dog is being exported to another country, and specific protocols exist for each country. Non-export titering is possible, but at present is not generally accepted as an alternative to vaccination by states or municipalities in the US. We will sometimes use a protective Rabies titer as supportive evidence of protection in a dog too sick to receive a vaccination, or one who has had a serious vaccine reaction in the past. How that result is interpreted should there be a bite or exposure to a rabid animal is up to state or municipal officials. However, when providing a waiver for Rabies vaccination, as is legal in a great number of states, it would seem prudent to measure a titer as verification of an immune response to previous vaccinations against Rabies (assuming previous vaccines have been performed).

Many veterinarians are resistant to titer testing, believing that there is no proof that the titer proves immunity. I personally find this puzzling, as we are more than comfortable using changes over time in antibody levels (titers) to diagnose disease or judge response to treatment. It is common practice to measure titers in humans vaccinated against rabies (such as veterinarians!) to determine the need for additional vaccinations. A measurable titer demonstrates that the dog's immune system has responded to the vaccine, and produced antibodies, the very cornerstone of immunity.

Other veterinarians oppose titer testing on the basis of cost and convenience, as a titer typically costs more than the vaccine. They are also usually sent out to a laboratory, so if a dog is determined to need an additional vaccine, the owner must make another trip to the veterinary hospital. While I respect such a veterinarian's concern for the client's finances and convenience, those factors should never be put ahead of recommending the best quality medical care available. Furthermore, this viewpoint does not take into consideration one very important fact – the decision to have a titer performed prior to any vaccination should be made by the owner, not the veterinarian.

Some veterinary experts recognize the crucial importance of memory cells as the foundation of immunity, and choose to use titers very selectively. They believe that if it is demonstrated that a dog produced a measurable titer following a vaccine, further titers are not necessary. They argue that in the absence of exposure to a virus, the antibody level may fall below prescribed parameters after many years. That does not mean the dog is not protected, as the memory cells are still present and can trigger antibody production if exposure to the virus occurs.

Currently, there are two general methods for using titer testing in a dog's preventative health plan. The first is to titer after initial vaccinations, and repeat the titer every one to three years, just as dogs were traditionally vaccinated in the past. This plan meets the requirements of many dog care facilities such as training centers, groomers, and boarding kennels. Most dogs will have protective titers for much of their lives, assuming their immune system is functioning normally.

The second method of utilizing titer testing is to titer after the initial series of vaccinations. If a protective titer is demonstrated, the competency of the immune system has been demonstrated, and no further titers are performed. This plan is based on the knowledge that the memory cells that induce antibody production will be present for the life of an immune-competent dog, even if antibody levels fall below laboratory minimums due to lack of natural exposure to disease.

While this viewpoint is certainly well grounded in the science of immunology, it does cause concern among both owners and some veterinarians, who worry when a dog's titer is less than laboratory minimums. Because of the questions that arise when antibodies levels are low, this method has not yet become universally accepted. However, it is noteworthy that Therapy Dogs International,® the largest therapy dog certification organization in the US, requires only a set of initial vaccinations for Therapy Dog registration – an unspoken concurrence with the concept that an initial vaccination series confers lifelong immunity.

Your dog's individual health needs and conditions, as well as the need for "proof" of immunity for third parties will factor in to your decision of which titering method to use. A realistic assessment of the risk of exposure versus the likely presence of adequate memory cells must be made should your dog's titer level falls below laboratory minimums. And of course, your dog's overall health, lifestyle, geographic location, etc., must be considered when deciding upon a preventative health program. Decisions about revaccination should be made based on scientific immunological fact and current knowledge of a specific vaccine's long-term efficacy.

Remember…

1. A titer measures your dog's antibody production in response to a vaccine.

2. Many experts consider a protective titer good for the life of the dog, based on the demonstrated competence of the immune system.

3. Many kennels, training centers, etc. will accept titers in lieu of vaccinations.

4. Titering for rabies is possible, but may not be legally accepted as an alternative to vaccination.

CHAPTER 5. VACCINATING YOUR DOG

Now that you have read this far, you have a good understanding of what vaccines are and how they work, as well as the common diseases against which your dog should be protected. You understand how titers can demonstrate that your dog's immune system has responded effectively to a vaccine, and prove additional vaccination is not necessary. Yet, if you are like many owners, you are still a bit unsure of exactly what vaccination protocol you should choose.

Given that the largest veterinary associations, veterinary colleges, and experts have been recommending extended vaccination protocols for many years, it is bewildering and dismaying to learn of dogs receiving yearly vaccinations. In fact, in the renowned veterinary textbook Kirk's Current Veterinary Therapy XI, published in 1992, authors Drs. Phipps and Schultz wrote, "A practice that was started many years ago and that lacks scientific validity or verification is annual revaccinations. Almost without exception there is no immunologic requirement for annual revaccination. Immunity to viruses persists for years or for the life of the animal." (page 205).

While some veterinarians are extremely progressive and incorporated extended vaccination protocols long ago, others still recommend yearly or non-essential vaccinations. Keep in mind as your dog's owner, you may accept or decline <u>any</u> recommendation. It is your right and responsibility to decide what is in your dog's best interest. The only vaccination you are legally obligated to give and keep current according to your state's law is rabies.

So, exactly which vaccinations should your dog receive, and when should they be given? In my practice I start with a basic vaccination schedule and modify it individually for each dog. Changes can be made as lifestyle circumstances change. Depending on the case, you may elect titer testing to measure the level of antibodies against disease, or to verify immune system competence after vaccination.

Dr. Coger's Core Vaccination Protocol

Age	Vaccine Type
10 weeks	Parvovirus (MLV)
14 weeks	DAP
18 weeks (optional)	DAP
22 weeks or older	Rabies, thimersol free
1 year post last vaccination	Distemper/Parvovirus titer
1 year post initials Rabies vaccination	Rabies 3 year, thimersol free

DAP: Distemper, adenovirus type 2, parvovirus

Do not administer more than one vaccine at a time.

Perform antibody titers for distemper and parvovirus every three years thereafter, if desired.

Vaccinate for rabies virus according to applicable laws, except where circumstances indicate it could be medically harmful and applicable laws allow a waiver. In these cases, a rabies antibody titer may also be performed to further demonstrate the immune status of the dog. Some states may require rabies vaccination prior to 22 weeks of age. In those cases, be sure to respect the four week interval between vaccines.

Consider non-core vaccines as are appropriate for your dog, as discussed in Chapter 3. If you elect to include non-core vaccines, follow the Best Practices for Vaccinating Dogs later in this chapter. Begin non-core vaccines four weeks after the last core vaccine was administered.

Note: My preference is not to vaccinate puppies younger than 10 weeks. They are well protected by maternally derived antibodies until 16 weeks or older, and may not be fully immunologically competent until at least 8 weeks of age. Many breeders will have puppies vaccinated at 8 weeks – if this has occurred prior to getting your puppies, the above recommended ages will need to be adjusted. Vaccinate at four week intervals.

Vaccinating the Adult Dog

Perhaps as you are reading this, you're wondering how to apply the protocol above to your adult dog who has been previously vaccinated, or you may be wondering about the adult dog that has just come into your home. What vaccinations should be done?

To determine this, you first need to review your dog's health history. Look back at what vaccinations your adult dog has received. If there have been two or more DAP or DP vaccines given, you can move to a titer. If records are incomplete, you may choose to titer and vaccinate only if titer results are inadequate, or administer a DAP and titer four weeks later. It really is as simple as that! Rabies must be given according to state laws, and it is likely your adult dog will already be on a three-year schedule. Non-core vaccines are of course considered on an individual basis, as described in Chapter 3.

Beyond the vaccination protocol and notes provided above, there are some "Best Practices" to follow when administering vaccines. Following these simple rules can minimize risk and maximize efficacy when a vaccine is given. I consider these simple rules the "second half" of my vaccination protocol, and urge you to follow them diligently.

Because dogs older than 14–16 wk of age should have a competent immune systems and are not likely to have interfering levels of maternal antibodies, administration of a single initial dose of an infectious (MLV or recombinant) vaccine can be expected to provide a protective immune response. It is common practice, however, in the US, to administer two doses, four weeks apart, to dogs without a history of prior vaccination. This is thought to maximize immunity in dogs that may have a sub-optimal response to the first vaccine. It would be equally acceptable to measure a titer four weeks after the first vaccination. If that titer result is adequate, the second vaccine would be considered unnecessary.

Best Practices for Vaccinating Dogs

1. In accordance with vaccine manufacturer's recommendations (i.e. the label), vaccinate only <u>healthy</u> dogs. If there is a health problem present, it should be treated, and the vaccine administered at a later date, when the dog has completely recovered.

2. If blood testing, such as a heartworm/Lyme/Ehrlichia/Anaplasmosis test or a complete blood count and biochemical profile is being run, be sure results are negative or normal before vaccinating the dog. If these tests are sent out to a laboratory, you can return later for any needed vaccines. Doing so will avoid unknowingly vaccinating unhealthy dogs.

3. Do not administer more than <u>one</u> vaccine at a time to <u>any</u> dog, especially those less than 33 pounds. Smaller dogs have a significantly higher risk of reaction when multiple vaccines are given at one time.

4. When spreading out vaccines, use a minimum 4-week interval.

5. Do not vaccinate at times of stress. While it may seem convenient to have vaccines given at the time of spaying or neutering, the physical and mental stress of general anesthesia and surgery, as well as the

administration of other drugs, makes vaccination at this time inappropriate. By similar logic, do not vaccinate during boarding, grooming, travelling, etc.

6. A puppy's initial vaccine is ideally administered no earlier than 8 weeks of age. The newest AAHA recommendations suggest not administering inactivated or killed vaccines before 12 weeks of age.

7. Do not vaccinate females in season. Hormonal changes can alter the normal response to vaccines.

8. Do not vaccinate pregnant dogs.

9. Do not vaccinate dogs with a history of adverse reactions.

10. Do not give five or seven way combo vaccinations. They are rarely indicated, and often are implicated in adverse reactions.

11. If giving non-core vaccines, begin after the core vaccines are given. Always vaccinate at four week intervals.

12. Utilize titer testing to verify response to previous vaccinations. Begin after the puppy series is completed, or after one vaccine in the case of the adult dog.

13. Consider giving vaccinations early in the day. In the event of an adverse reaction, your veterinary office will still be open, rather than having to visit an emergency clinic.

CHAPTER 6. ADVERSE REACTIONS

As you remember from reading the introduction, vaccine reactions can take place immediately after a vaccination is given. Lucy, one of the dogs who inspired me to write this book, suffered a very severe immediate hypersensitivity reaction. This is a similar type of reaction to that suffered by people allergic to bee stings. However, there are other kinds of vaccine reactions that take more time to occur, and may not even be recognized as reactions by many veterinarians. My own dog, Piper, upon receiving his first rabies vaccination, experienced a delayed type reaction. The onset of the reaction was several weeks after vaccination. While not fatal, this reaction challenged his health for over the first year of his life.

It should be emphasized that most dogs do not suffer adverse reactions from vaccines. The vast majority of dogs develop protective levels of immunity to disease from the first vaccines administered, and suffer no ill effects. But for those who do suffer an adverse reaction, the effects can be life altering, or life ending.

The most commonly recognized adverse reaction to vaccination is an immediate hypersensitivity reaction. Typically affected dogs will experience facial swelling, or even whole body hives. Interference with breathing may occur. The onset of the reaction is usually within minutes to hours after vaccination. Dogs experiencing such a reaction should of course be seen immediately by a veterinarian. In many cases, administration of an antihistamine such as diphenhydramine (Benedryl®) can slow the reaction. Be sure to discuss this with your veterinarian prior to administration, and for the right dose for your dog.

Dogs suffering this type of immediate reaction are usually treated with corticosteroids, and recover uneventfully. However, this reaction is a "red flag" that the dog's body is sensitive to some or all of the ingredients in the vaccine. Obviously, the vaccine should not be administered to the dog again, for fear of causing an even more severe reaction. Extreme caution should be used with any other vaccines as well.

Some veterinarians have adopted the practice of pre-medicating dogs that have experienced previous vaccine reactions with diphenhydramine (Benedryl®) prior to giving a vaccine. This practice is thought to block the vaccine reaction, when in reality it simply masks the symptoms. The body is still being exposed to a product it is "allergic" to. I personally find this practice unjustifiable, indefensible, and contrary to the best interests of the patient. This is especially true in the case of diseases to which dog is already immune from previous vaccines, or non-core diseases to which the dog's exposure is low.

Other types of acute adverse reactions occur 24 to 72 hours after vaccination. The most frequent is swelling or soreness at the injection site, especially common with Rabies and Lyme vaccines. Other dogs may suffer from fevers, lethargy, vomiting, diarrhea, stiffness, or sore joints. More serious reactions include neurologic disorders including encephalitis, and autoimmune problems such as autoimmune hemolytic anemia (AIHA), where the immune system destroys the red blood cells, and immune mediated thrombocytopenia (ITP), where platelets are destroyed. Both of these autoimmune diseases, which can appear as acute or delayed type reactions, can be fatal.

Delayed type reactions usually occur 7 to 45 days after vaccination. Many veterinarians overlook vaccination reaction as a cause for these problems because of the time interval from vaccination. These cases often appear as a chronic disease problem – in my dog Piper, the main physical sign was daily profuse, intractable diarrhea, unresponsive to treatment. Secondary effects were weight loss, inability to gain weight, and extreme anxiety and inability to focus.

Treatment of delayed type reactions can be more problematic than in more immediate reactions. As already mentioned, many times the problem is not recognized as a vaccine reaction. In fact, I did not consider a delayed vaccine reaction as a cause for Piper's health problems at first. Rather, I looked for the more common causes to explain his symptoms, and worked through a variety of conventional treatments, dietary changes, and natural treatments. Despite using everything I knew at the time, I could not stop his daily diarrhea or put any weight on his too-thin frame. It was not until I enlisted the assistance of a veterinarian trained in homeopathy that I was able to help him. The lesson I learned from Piper was that should a dog suffer any health issue within a couple months of receiving a vaccination, the question must be put forward, "Could this possibly be a vaccine reaction?" The term "vaccinosis" is now often used instead of adverse reaction to describe long term illness or compromised health secondary to vaccination, especially in dogs which have had multiple vaccinations.

Certain breeds seem to be more prone to vaccine reactions, and also seem to be more commonly afflicted with autoimmune diseases such as AIHA or ITP. Dr. Jean Dodds, one of the foremost vaccine researchers in the world, notes that the breeds "...Akita, American Cocker Spaniel, German

Shepherd, Golden Retriever, Irish Setter, Great Dane, Kerry Blue Terrier, Weimeraner, and all Dachshund and Poodle varieties..." seem predisposed to autoimmune type adverse effects. She also observed that breeds with white coat color or coat color dilutions seem more prone to react. Dr. Dodds and other researchers found the same breeds listed above appeared susceptible to other types of adverse vaccine reactions, particularly post-vaccinal seizures, high fevers, and painful episodes of hypertrophic osteodystrophy (HOD). I believe it is very important to be aware of the health predispositions of your dog's breed, and to discuss them with your veterinarian prior to any vaccination or other procedure or treatment.

The most feared type of adverse reaction is vaccination site cancer. The most commonly occurring such cancer is the fibrosarcoma. Usually thought of as a reaction to the carrier and/or adjuvant included in the vaccine, these tumors are seen more often in cats than dogs. However researchers in Italy have found distinct similarities between dog and cat fibrosarcomas associated with injection sites. These tumors can be very invasive, growing rapidly and deeply into the tissues and bone, far beyond the possibility of surgical removal. They also tend to regrow quickly, even if a surgical excision appears complete. Non-surgical therapies are generally unsuccessful.

Any abnormality, even the most mild, noted after a vaccination should be brought to your veterinarian's attention, whether it occurs minutes or weeks after the injection. If it is determined to possibly be a vaccine reaction, it should be reported to the manufacturer, who in turn must provide that information to government regulatory bodies. Unfortunately, many adverse events are not reported to veterinarians let alone vaccine manufacturers, making true safety data of specific vaccine products potentially inflated.

Treatment of vaccine reactions will vary according to the symptoms present. Many holistic veterinarians will use homeopathic remedies such as thuja prior to and following a vaccine, as a combination of prevention and treatment. While this is not in accordance with the traditional practice of homeopathy, many consider it helpful. Other veterinarians will treat only symptomatic reactions, and will use conventional and/or natural medicines.

Should your dog experience a vaccine reaction, be sure to discuss all options with your veterinarian before you choose a treatment plan, beyond any obvious emergency treatment needed. You may want to consider consulting a veterinarian practicing homeopathy, herbal, or other alternative medicine methods, or one who integrates alternative techniques with traditional medicine (see the References section for links to aid in your search for alternative or integrative veterinarians). Be sure the notation of the reaction is placed prominently in your dog's medical record. It is likely that you will elect to never give your dog the vaccine that caused the reaction again, and proceed cautiously with any other vaccinations, following the Best Practices for Vaccination outlined in the previous chapter.

Remember...

1. Any abnormality following vaccination should be addressed promptly with your veterinarian.

2. Adverse reactions can occur immediately, or weeks to months after vaccination. They can be life threatening, regardless of when they occur.

3. A variety of approaches can be used to treat vaccine reactions, including conventional, herbal, homeopathic, and other alternative techniques.

Piper, enjoying the snow after his recovery.

CHAPTER 7. PARTING THOUGHTS

One of the most important things I tell my clients is, "Your dog's health is ultimately your responsibility." Whether to accept a veterinarian's recommendation is an owner's choice – especially if you have unanswered questions or information that conflicts with that recommendation. Do not be afraid to decline a vaccination (or other treatment) until all of your questions have been answered. Do not hesitate to seek a second opinion, or to consult with a veterinary specialist or holistic veterinarian. And, if your current veterinarian does not meet your needs, do not be afraid to search out to a veterinarian who does.

Our knowledge of vaccines and immunology has greatly progressed in recent years. The days of the yearly "booster shot" are long behind us! In my opinion and experience, there simply is no scientific justification for giving core vaccines (other than rabies in accordance with state laws) more than once or twice in the average dog's lifetime. Studies have suggested that immunity from commonly used vaccinations lasts seven years or even more. <u>There is no benefit to giving an additional vaccination to the dog that already has sufficient immunity.</u>

As noted by Dr. Schultz, "In our studies, puppies vaccinated annually with modified live CPV-2, (parvovirus) CDV, (distemper) and CAV (adenovirus) vaccines received no added benefit from annual revaccination throughout a period of 7 years when compared to dogs that were vaccinated as puppies then challenged with virulent virus at 7 years of age. Both groups of dogs were protected from challenge infection with CPV-2, CDV and/or CAV." (R.D. Schultz, "Considerations in Designing Effective and Safe Vaccination Programs for Dogs," May 2000.) Yes, you read that correctly! That study, published in 2000, showed a 7 year duration of effectiveness for a DAP vaccine. Yet today as I write this, dogs are still being given that vaccine on a yearly basis, with no benefit, potential unnecessary risk, and needless cost to their owners.

Many experts consider repeated vaccinations as a cause of many health problems, from immediate hypersensitivity reactions like anaphylaxis, hives, and facial swelling, to autoimmune destruction of red blood cells or platelets, neurologic disorders, bone and joint problems, hypothyroidism and more. All of these problems can have life impacting or threatening consequences. When you consider that in many cases the dog was already immune to the disease against which he was being vaccinated, it becomes obvious that inappropriate vaccination is contrary to the basic tenet of all medicine: *Primum non nocere* --first, do no harm.

"He is your friend, your partner, your defender, your dog. You are his life, his love, his leader. He will be yours, faithful and true, to the last beat of his heart. You owe it to him to be worthy of such devotion." - Author Unknown

Your dog's health is ultimately your responsibility.

REFERENCES

Key Websites

Dr. Coger's Book Website:

www.VaccinesExplained.com

> Contains references, news, and links to relevant information

> Download a sample health record

> Book a consultation with Dr. Coger

Rabies Challenge Fund:

http://www.rabieschallengefund.org/

> The Rabies Challenge Fund Charitable Trust will determine the duration of immunity conveyed by rabies vaccines. The goal is to extend the required interval for rabies boosters to 5 and then to 7 years.

American Animal Hospital Association Vaccine Guidelines

https://www.aahanet.org/library/caninevaccine.aspx

Organizations and Veterinary Resources

The organizations listed below all have search functions on their sites to help you find a veterinarian near you, the majority of which support minimal or extended vaccination protocols. Many are experienced in handling adverse vaccine reactions and vaccinosis cases.

The American Holistic Veterinary Medical Association

http://www.ahvma.org

The Academy of Veterinary Homeopathy

http://www.theavh.org

Veterinary Botanical Medical Association

http://www.vbma.org

American Veterinary Medical Association

http://www.avma.org

Veterinary Institute of Integrative Medicine

http://www.viim.org/

Scholarly Papers

Schultz, RD, Thiel, B, Mukhtar, E, Sharp, P, Larson, LJ. Age and Long Term Protective Immunity in Dogs and Cats. J. Comp. Path. 2010. Vol. 142, S102-S108.

Schultz, RD. Duration of Immunity for Canine and Feline Vaccines: A Review. Veterinary Microbiology 117(2006) 75 – 79.

Schultz, RD. Considerations in Designing Effective and Safe Vaccination Programs for Dogs. In: Recent Advances in Canine Infectious Diseases, Carmichael, L. E. (Ed.) Pub. International Veterinary Information Service. 5 May 2000.

Smith CA. Current concepts - Are We Vaccinating Too Much? J Am Vet Med Assoc 1995; 207(4):421-425.

Phillips TR, Schultz RD. Canine and Feline Vaccines. In: Kirk RW, Bonagura JD, eds. Kirk's Current Veterinary Therapy XI. Philadelphia: WB Saunders Co, 1992; 202-206.

Dodds WJ. More Bumps on the Vaccine Road. In: Schultz RD, ed. Advances in Veterinary Medicine 41: Veterinary Vaccines and Diagnostics. San Diego: Academic Press, 1999; 715-732.

Moore, GE, Glickman, LT. A Perspective on Vaccine Guidelines and Titer Tests for Dogs. JAVMA, Vol 224, No. 2, 200-203. Jan 15, 2004.

Moore, GE, HogenEsch, H. Adverse Vaccinal Events in Dogs and Cats. Vet Clinics Small Animal 40 (20120) 393-407. 2010.

Moore, G, Guptill, LF, Ward, MP, Glickman, NW, Faunt, KK, Lewis, HB, Glickman, LT. Adverse events diagnosed within three days of vaccine administration in dogs. JAVMA Oct 2005, Vol. 227, No. 7, 1102-1108

Popular Reading

These publications contain good information on a variety of natural health topics, including vaccinations.

The Whole Dog Journal

http://www.whole-dog-journal.com

Dogs Naturally Magazine

http://www.dogsnaturallymagazine.com

Animal Wellness Magazine
http://www.animalwellnessmagazine.com

ABOUT THE AUTHOR

Dr. Laurie S. Coger's interest in animals began early in life. Growing up in a rural area of New York State, she spent her childhood with both dogs and horses. A career in veterinary medicine was her aspiration from an early age. She graduated with honors from Cornell University's College of Agriculture & Life Sciences, majoring in Animal Science, with a special interest and advanced training in animal nutrition. She received her DVM degree from Cornell's College of Veterinary Medicine. As she began her veterinary private practice career, she continued her interest in show and performance dogs. She has successfully competed in conformation, obedience, and herding events, achieving many titles with her dogs.

She often provides on-site veterinary care at dog competitions and events, with the combined perspective of a competitor and a veterinarian. She is a frequent speaker at dog events, and has served as both the obedience and veterinary section editor for an award winning national magazine, the Australian Shepherd Journal, as well as writing for other magazines and blogs.

Dr. Coger's practice philosophy emphasizes natural methods and care. She regularly integrates chiropractic, low level laser, herbal, nutritional, and physical therapy techniques into her treatment plans. She is a staunch advocate of educating and empowering owners to make proactive, informed decisions for their dog's health.

*Visit
www.VaccinesExplained.com
for news and more vaccine
information.*

Made in the USA
Lexington, KY
07 June 2014